WARNINGS!

END TIMES
SCENARIOS

DIANE BISH

DEDICATION

*This book
is dedicated to those who lost their lives in the terrible
disaster of 9/11. Many people thought such an apocalyptic
event could never happen...
but it did.*

INTRODUCTION

*A*s a concert organist and host of *The Joy of Music International Televisions Series*, it has been my privilege for over 30 years to travel worldwide in the making of over 500 programs from the great organs and cathedrals of the world.

Since traveling on planes and waiting in airports is mostly "downtime," I have chosen to take the opportunity to read: newspapers, books, magazines, the internet, and my favorite, the Bible.

Rather than being a reader of fiction, I prefer "reality reading," with a fascination for biographies, history, contemporary events and news. I am interested in reading about events that have taken place in the past and also those predictions of things to come. For me, these predictions of current and future events are known as prophesies, given to us in scripture by God himself, through divinely inspired prophets and apostles.

In these days, it is almost impossible to pick up a newspaper in one hand and a Bible in another, and not see the amazing correlation of things taking place today that have been precisely prophesied thousands of years ago.

Just as God has prophesied, these end-time disasters and scenarios are now happening in unprecedented frequency and intensity, not only in the United States, but around the world.

It is almost certain, that you, or someone you know, will experience one or more of these end-time disasters now or in the days to come. They are already upon us, if only we have the eyes to see and the ears to hear.

The individuals in this book of End Time Scenarios are people like you and me, some who are ready to meet God, some who are not. Through God's own hand, through prophets and through the words of Jesus, we are warned to "be ready, for the Son of Man will come at an hour you do not expect!"

In these days of dire warnings and catastrophes' throughout the earth, it is imperative that each and every person hear the life-changing good news of the gospel and accept this wonderful Jesus who will be with us in this life and in eternity to come.

Diane Bish
October, 2012

CONTENTS

WARNINGS

MATTHEW 25: 44

*"Watch therefore, for you do not know what hour your
Lord is coming.
Therefore you also be ready, for the Son of Man is coming
at an hour you do not expect."*

*Mark 13:35-37
"Take heed, watch and pray; for you do not know when
the time is.
Watch therefore, for you do not know when the
Master of the house is coming—
In the evening, at midnight, at the crowing of the rooster,
or in the morning—
Lest, coming suddenly, he find you sleeping
And what I say to you, I say to all:
WATCH!"*

Warnings are a part of everyday life: poison,
do not swallow; danger; flammable under pressure;
watch your step; smoking may be hazardous to your
health; don't drink and drive; stop, railroad crossing;
poison, keep away from eyes...

Most people take heed to these warnings!

WHY?

Because they keep us from danger.

In the Bible, God has given us numerous warnings.
They are written plainly throughout scripture.
These warnings are given out of God's great love
for each and all people.

WHY?

Because God loves us so much that He wants to keep us
from harm, sorrow, heartache, disaster, and even death.

In end-time scenarios and apocalyptic events,
God also is warning us to be ready to meet him.

If we heed these warnings, we will be safe,
both in this life and the life to come.

In Daniel 5, an amazing story is told of a specific warning given directly by the Hand of God. It is written to King Belshazzar, for his rebellious heart toward the Almighty.

"King Belshazzar gave a great banquet for a thousand of his nobles and drank wine with them. While Belshazzar was drinking his wine, he gave orders to bring in the gold and silver goblets that Nebuchadnezzar his father had taken from the temple in Jerusalem, so that the King and his nobles, his wives and his concubines might drink from them. As they drank the wine, they praised the gods of gold and silver, of bronze, iron, wood and stone. Suddenly the fingers of a human hand appeared and wrote on the plaster of the wall, near the lampstand in the royal palace. The king watched the hand as it wrote. His face turned pale and he was so frightened that his knees knocked together and his legs gave way.
Daniel the prophet and interpreter of dreams was called upon to tell the king what the writing meant. Daniel came before the king and gave his explanation:
O Belshazzar, you have not humbled yourself, though you knew all these things. Instead, you have set yourself up against the Lord of Heaven. You had the goblets from his temple brought to you. You praised the gods of silver and gold, of bronze, iron, wood and stone, which cannot see or hear or understand. But you did not honor the God who holds in His hand your life and all your ways. Therefore, He sent the hand that wrote in the inscription:

MENE, MENE, TEKEL, PARSIN

*God has numbered the days of your reign
and brought it to an end!
You have been weighed on the scales and found wanting!*

Your kingdom is divided and given to the
Medes and Persians!
THAT VERY NIGHT, BELSHAZZAR,
KING OF THE BABYLONIANS WAS SLAIN
AND DARIOUS THE MEDE TOOK OVER
THE KINGDOM!"

Many times throughout history, God has given
His warnings through earthquake and fire,
wind and water, drought and pestilence.

SO IT IS IN THE END TIMES:

THEN SHALL YOU HEAR OF WARS
AND RUMORS OF WARS,
NATION WILL RISE AGAINST NATION, AND
KINGDOM AGAINST KINGDOM,
THERE WILL BE FAMINES AND EARTHQUAKES IN
VARIOUS PLACES.
ALL THESE ARE THE BEGINNINGS OF SORROWS.
FOR THEN THERE WILL BE GREAT DISTRESS,
UNEQUALED FROM THE BEGINNING OF THE
WORLD UNTIL NOW—AND NEVER TO BE
EQUALED AGAIN.

NOW LEARN THIS LESSON FROM THE FIG TREE;
AS SOON AS IT'S TWIGS GET TENDER AND IT'S
LEAVES COME OUT, YOU KNOW THAT SUMMER
IS NEAR. EVEN SO, WHEN YOU SEE ALL THESE
THINGS, YOU KNOW THAT IT IS NEAR,
RIGHT AT THE DOOR.
THEREFORE, KEEP WATCH, AND BE READY
BECAUSE YOU DO NOT KNOW ON WHAT DAY
YOUR LORD WILL COME."

WARS AND RUMORS OF WARS

MATTHEW 24, 6, 14,42

*"IN THE LAST DAYS THERE SHALL BE WARS
AND RUMORS OF WARS,
NATION WILL RISE AGAINST NATION AND KINGDOM
AGAINST KINGDOM."*

*"AND THIS GOSPEL OF THE KINGDOM WILL BE
PREACHED IN THE WHOLE WORLD AS A TESTIMONY
TO ALL NATIONS AND THEN THE END WILL COME."*

*"SO YOU ALSO MUST BE READY,
FOR YOU KNOW NOT THE HOUR WHEN
THE SON OF MAN WILL COME."*

Claire was once again back in a war zone. As a correspondent for NBC News, she had worked for several years in Iraq until she was forced to return home to face a battle with lung cancer. After several years of constant struggle with the disease, she was finally in remission and was now in Afghanistan to once again serve the United States in a war-torn country. She had been asked to report on alarming killings of American and British soldiers by Afghan army and police trainees. It was a dangerous mission, but she had experienced such things before, and she was just glad to be healthy and back at work.

In the two years that she had struggled with cancer, she had had many hours to reflect and ponder on war, the world situation, and her own personal life. She had experienced many terrible events in Iraq: killing and maiming of civilians, soldiers broken in both body and spirit, cities bombed, and families killed and separated. It all was so heartbreaking, and she kept asking herself: "Why??"

"Why are there so many wars and rumors of wars around the world?" she often thought. It seemed more than ever there was turmoil in every part of the earth. Israel planning to bomb Iran. Iran vowing to obliterate Israel. Governments killing civilians by the hundreds of thousands in Sudan. Shiites hating Sunnis. Palestinians seeking revenge on their enemies; Syrian leaders murdering thousands of innocents.

However, as she meditated on war, she also thought about individual people. They fight, they hate, they kill, they quarrel, and they demand vengeance and retaliation. Countries, she often thought, are made up of individuals, so it was understandable that there would be terrible and constant war and bloodshed. She was sick about it all, and even when she looked into her own heart, she felt many of these same emotions that she detested in others. "Where could I ever find true peace and fulfillment?" she often thought, but as of yet, she hadn't discovered it.

In the two weeks she had been in Afghanistan, she had become good friends with Bryan Milstrom, a young soldier, who himself had only been in the country for several weeks. They had been going on trips to visit army outposts outside the city of Kabul. He was light-hearted and even innocent in spirit. With many chances to talk and share, they had acquired a bond of trust and confidence in each other, and Claire was thankful for a friend who would look out for her in such a dangerous place.

She had noticed that he was different in some way, and in just a short time she had come to know why. After a meal one evening, they sat down together and he told her how, after a very troubled life, a friend had shared with him the gospel of Christ and how life changing it was. In time, he too, surrendered his life to Jesus Christ, and found a joy and peace in living that he had never known before.

"I am confident and unafraid," he told Claire. "No matter the situation or circumstances around me, I am at peace because I know Jesus is with me now, and even for eternity. And I have true meaning in living."

"Do you have that same peace, Claire?" he asked with great caring.

"No, I don't, I'm sorry to say," Claire responded. "All my life I have looked for something to fill my soul—to give me true meaning and fulfillment. I would like to know this Jesus and the peace you're talking about."

"Why don't we pray together, Claire," Bryan asked. "The Bible says that 'now is the day of salvation' and that Christ is continually knocking on the door of your heart. If you open the door to Him, he will come in and live in your heart."

That night, they prayed together, something she had never done alone or with another person. She followed his leadership as he prayed and she repeated his words.

"Lord, I thank you that you love me," he prayed.

"Lord, I thank you that you love me," Claire responded.

"Please forgive my sin, come into my heart, and make me a new person."

"Please forgive my sin, come into my heart, and make me a new person."

"I accept you as my lord and savior."

"I accept you as my lord and savior."

"Thank you for giving me salvation."

"Thank you for giving me salvation."

"In Jesus name, I pray."

"In Jesus name, I pray."

"Amen."

"Amen."

In that special moment, and in the following days in the midst of work and continuous danger, Claire felt a strange warmth and joy that she had never known before, just like Bryan had said. She knew now that Christ lived within her, and that she had a new beginning with meaning and purpose. She wanted to tell everyone, including her own family, what had happened—especially her mother.

It had been a week since she had prayed with Bryan that night. She had been sending reports and videos back to her Washington office about life on the front lines. Although it was her job, she still felt this and all wars were terrible and fruitless. So many tragedies, killings and heartbreak. It pained her heart.

The morning of September 27, she and several other journalists joined Bryan and a platoon of twenty men, including three Afghan trainees on patrol in a town seventy-five miles out of Kabul. She was a bit anxious, but not really afraid. Accompanied by Humvees and unmanned drones overhead, they were suddenly informed by radio of problems ahead. They were being followed by people walking along the rooftops as they traveled slowly through the streets. One of the officers in the platoon suddenly shouted of imminent danger, but before they could run for cover, both the armed rooftop enemies and two of the three Afghan trainees turned on the platoon and the accompanying journalists.

"Run, fast!" Bryan screamed, "Inside, anywhere." He turned instinctively to Claire nearby, grabbed her arm, and along with the others, dashed for cover. They ran for a nearby wall and hunkered down in a corner section of the bombed-out building. Suddenly, there was an explosion of enormous strength—-the wall had been rigged, perhaps detonated by a mobile device. Flying shrapnel and projectiles ripped into the soldiers and journalists. Bryan's left leg was shattered and his head was bleeding profusely. Along with the others, Claire had been injured badly and was not able to move. She cried out to Bryan—-there was no answer. A medic, a member of the platoon, ran quickly to Claire, trying to stop the bleeding from all over her body. Another soldier raced to the side of Bryan, whose bones were shattered along with tendons in the legs and arms. His head continued to bleed. His face was pale and body limp—-it was too late.

The medic and six other platoon members carried the wounded to one of the waiting Humvees and headed to the nearest treatment center. Claire was in serious condition and needed to be attended to immediately. The medic knew local hospitals and aid stations would not be able to save her life. By the end of the day, a military helicopter with doctors aboard flew with Claire and several others to a plane waiting to fly the severely wounded to the U. S. military hospital in Landstuhl, Germany. Military staff and doctors on board kept Claire alive until she reached the airport at Ramstein, Germany.

At the airport, a group of nurses, doctors and attendants were waiting for the wounded. A chaplain spoke to each person individually, and finally came to Claire.

"Claire, you don't have to worry now," he spoke in soft tones. "You are in Germany." His hands then formed the sign of the cross. Claire was whisked away to the U.S. military hospital at Landstuhl and was immediately taken to ICU— where every minute counted.

The doctors at the hospital confered and decide Claire's family should be notified immediately of the seriousness of her condition.

Claire's mother, Daren, a divorcee of over twenty years, lived alone. Claire was the love of her life and Daren had missed her so much since she left for Afghanistan. She had spent many sleepless nights worrying about the safety of her beloved and only daughter.

Daren was at the breakfast table when the call came in from the hospital in Germany. The news of Claire's condition came as a knife into her heart. She didn't know if she could bear it.

Immediately canceling everything for the week, Daren was able to secure a flight to Germany that very night.

Arriving at the Landstuhl hospital the next afternoon, Daren walked into the room, pale and trembling from worry and sleeplessness.

"Claire, I'm here," her mother said, touching her feverish forehead.

Claire, opening her eyes slightly, responded weakly.

"Oh mother, I am so glad to see you," she sobbed. "I'm so sorry it's like this."

Daren embraced her daughter with all the love and warmth she possessed. How she loved Claire. "She is so beautiful, so talented, so kind and loyal," she thought.

They were together quietly for some time, realizing the gravity of the moment.

Suddenly, Claire's eyes opened and she gazed lovingly at her mother. She spoke, this time in a clearer and steadier voice.

"Mother, I want to share something with you—may I?"

"Of course, honey," her mother replied. "What is it?"

"Well, all my life you have loved me so much, and given me all you can, but something has been missing." She continued with great difficulty.

"My life has been so full in many ways, but—but my soul has been empty. I have searched, but never found the answer. I met a friend here, a young soldier named Bryan. One evening he told me about Jesus, who loved me and died for me. He said Jesus had changed his life and given him meaning and purpose. He asked me if I would like to know this Jesus, too," she paused, struggling to form the words.

"Mother, we prayed together, and I asked forgiveness for my sins and asked Jesus to come into my life. I don't know if I am dying now, but I want you to know that at last I'm at peace and my soul is filled—-I'm ready to go."

Daren's eyes filled with tears, and she placed her hand on Claire's fragile body.

Claire breathed heavily, but then uttered something she thought she would never say.

"Mother, please forgive me for asking—-but why didn't you ever tell me about Jesus? You gave me everything else, but somehow left out the most important thing."

Emotional pain covered Daren's face.

"I guess I didn't tell you because....because I didn't know Him myself. Maybe I never thought it was important… enough."

"Mother, will you pray with me," Claire softly pleaded. "You can ask Jesus to come into your life, too, just as I have....please."

"Yes, Claire, that would mean everything to me."

"Mother, just repeat after me, please, just as I did with Bryan. I hope I can make it through the words."

"Jesus," said Claire.

"Jesus," her mother said softly as she held Claire's hand

tightly.

"Please forgive me of my sins."

"Please forgive me of my sins."

"I ask you to come into my life as Lord and Savior."

"I ask you to come into my life as Lord and Savior."

"Thank you for hearing my prayer."

"Thank you for hearing my prayer."

"In Jesus name, I pray."

"In Jesus name I pray."

"Amen."

"Amen."

The silence was sacred.

"Oh, mother, I love you so much," Claire whispered. "Now we shall always be together, even for eternity. I have never been so happy…" Her words trailed off.

"Me too, Claire."

"Just one more thing, mother," Claire said with an even stronger voice. "Please tell my brother about Jesus…soon… before it's too late."

Claire's eyes closed, her pulse lowered. She was in perfect peace.

Her mother, laying her head on the arm of Claire, wept uncontrollably.

Philippians 1, 21
"For me to live is Christ, and to die is gain."

John 11:25
"I am the resurrection and the life: he that believeth in me, though he were dead, yet shall he live."

Revelation 21: 4

"And God will wipe away every tear from their eyes: there shall be no more death, nor sorrow, nor crying. There shall be no more pain, for the former things have passed away."

LOVERS OF SELF, MONEY, PLEASURE

2 TIMOTHY 3:1-5

BUT KNOW THIS:

"IN THE LAST DAYS, THERE WILL BE
TERRIBLE TIMES.
PEOPLE WILL BE LOVERS OF THEMSELVES,
LOVERS OF MONEY, BOASTFUL, PROUD, ABUSIVE,
DISOBEDIENT, UNGRATEFUL, UNHOLY,
WITHOUT LOVE, UNFORGIVING, SLANDEROUS,
WITHOUT SELF-CONTROL, BRUTAL, NOT LOVERS
OF THE GOOD, TREACHEROUS, RASH, CONCEITED,
LOVERS OF PLEASURE RATHER THAN
LOVERS OF GOD."

MARK 8;36

"FOR WHAT DOTH IT PROFIT A MAN,
IF HE GAIN THE WHOLE WORLD
AND LOSE HIS OWN SOUL."

It had been a bad twenty-four hours. Garrett had awakened early after a sleepless night, eaten a quick breakfast and jumped into his own car to make the forty-five minute ride to his office. Usually he was driven by a chauffeur, but not this morning. He was too upset and wanted to speak to no one.

For three days the weather had been severe and dangerous. Downpours and winds raged like Garrett had never experienced, but the chance to be alone with his own thoughts was what he needed this morning, as he drove through the perilous storms.

"That interview yesterday," he thought. "That's what kept me awake for most of the night!" Of course, he had endured many interviews during his life, hundreds even, and he was tired of the same questions: How did you begin? Who influenced you? How have you handled your amazing success? Ad infinitum.

However, yesterday was different. That insistent interviewer kept asking about his faith….what did he believe… did he ever read the Bible…what did he think about Jesus… did he think there was a heaven….did he think he would go there?

"Well to tell the truth," he thought, "I don't have a personal faith and in fact, I don't care to have one." Wasn't he one of the most successful and influential entrepreneurs in the world, and certainly one of the only multi-billionaires. He had done it all himself, and he didn't need God. "People who need God," he thought as he drove through the tumultuous weather, "are weak and incompetent." They needed something to lean on, and he didn't.

He finally arrived at his office, feeling no better than when he left the house.

The Bates office building was a 30-story monument of

steel and glass. It housed over one thousand employees, from secretaries to the brightest minds in the high-tech world. Not every employee knew Garrett Bates well, but those who did were well aware of his angry moods and tirades. They knew to keep their distance when he was mad and upset.

Mary Alden, his secretary of twenty years, could see that this was a day to stay clear of Mr. Bates. His arrival at his posh and immaculate office was not a happy one, as he frowned and grumbled to everyone on the way in. For a man with so much to be thankful for, Mary marveled at his angry countenance and hot temper. He was a brilliant man, but short-tempered and revengeful with anyone who disagreed with his opinion or stood in the way of his success and money.

For Garrett, the day continued as it had started, full of frustration and rankled feelings. He was a bit ashamed of himself, but always was able to blame others for things that he knew were his fault.

His general manager and good friend, Bill Mason, had asked to meet with Garrett that afternoon. Bill was a good and honest man, and had worked his way up to one of the top positions in the company. Unfortunately for Garrett, Bill was a devout Christian, and although they had become good friends, Garrett was highly annoyed at Bill's constant upbeat attitude, even when things were going badly. After his terribly upsetting interview the day before, Garrett was not pleased to meet with another person who might bring up the subject of personal faith and Jesus.

Bill, as usual, was right on time to the meeting and came in with a cheery smile.

"Good morning, Garrett," Bill said, as they shook hands. "How is your day going? It's pretty awful weather out there, isn't it?"

Garrett agreed, and told his friend of the difficult drive he had made to work that morning.

"You don't usually drive yourself, do you Garrett," Bill observed. "It would have been much more relaxing to ride in the limousine!"

"Yes, I know," Garrett responded, "but I wanted to be by myself. I had a bad night and an even worse yesterday. I had to deal with my anger."

"What happened, Garrett, if you don't mind my asking?"

"Nothing that you would probably find upsetting, Bill, but it really got to me!"

"This lady came to the house, an interviewer from some magazine, I don't even know the name, and instead of asking me questions about my work and success, she started asking me about my personal faith, and Jesus, and all that 'religious' stuff. It made me so angry that it kept me awake all night." Garrett's tone became increasingly irritable.

"You know, Bill, I'm not always the nicest guy around, but I'm not a bad guy. I run a world-wide company, with thousands of employees. I'm practically the founder of the high-tech world; I have more projects and problems than I know what to do with, and I don't have time to waste on 'where I'm going to spend eternity,' 'what do I think about Jesus,' and 'do I read the Bible'....it's just not important!" His voice raised in pitch and intensity.

"We have work to do here, Bill! I can't burden my mind with such irrelevant things as heaven and hell and whatever else!" he screamed.

Bill Mason was thoughtfully silent.

"I'm sorry to be bothering you today, Garrett, but I do have something eternal and relevant on my mind at the moment. I haven't told you, but my wife is dying of cancer. We don't know how many days she has to live. We are both Christians, and believers in Jesus Christ, so we know that whatever happens....I mean, when she passes away...that she'll be in heaven with her Lord and Savior. What I came to meet with you about is to ask if I could take a week off to be with my wife in these...perhaps, final days."

Garrett's face turned red with rage. "How could this happen," he thought. "Two days of Jesus, and faith, and heaven and eternity." He never wanted to hear another word about it. What did it have to do with his life anyway? Nothing! Nothing!

He exploded in anger.

"How can you even ask me for a week off in the earnings season!" he shouted. "We have projects and budgets and work that needs to be done and you're in charge of it all." He stomped across the room.

"There's a lot of money at stake here, Bill...probably billions!" he stormed. "And please, don't say anything more about where your wife's going to spend eternity. I don't want to hear it....do you understand!"

The room was silent. It was as if a knife had slashed into Bill's heart. He could hardly bring himself to speak.

"I'm sorry, Garrett," Bill said, with trembling in his voice. "I certainly didn't mean to be presumptuous...but there are things in life that are more important than money... and markets...and earnings season." He hesitated, trying to regain his composure.

"If I'm not able to have the time off, then I feel I should resign from the company as of today. It is imperative that I spend these final days with my precious wife."

Bill got up from his chair and headed toward the door, stopping at the entrance. Attempting to contain his tears and crushed feelings, Bill turned toward his friend of many years:

"You know, Garrett, there will come a day when you, and all of us, will have to think about eternity whether we want to or not. We will all stand before the judgment seat of God and give an account of what we did with Jesus. Did we ignore him, reject him, or accept him as Lord and Savior. He died for us, and for you, Garrett. God loves you with an everlasting love." He paused, looking straight into Garrett's eyes.

"My wife and I love you, too. I'm sure that she would like to tell you herself, but that probably won't be possible....now. Thanks for your time."

Garrett, stunned by the conversation, could not bring himself to say goodbye or give any words of apology. His head dropped to the desk with his hands covering his face. He was a miserable man with everything, yet nothing....with great riches, but poor within...with thousands of employees, but alone and lost.

Garrett knew he had to get out of his office before he exploded again in rage. He quickly packed his briefcase and headed for home, speaking to no one on the way out.

The weather had worsened since his morning drive. Many cars were stopped along the road with visibility at zero. The hills and valleys of northern California that he knew so well were now completely invisible to the eye, blocked by driving wind and rain. Not able to see the road ahead, he drove on, his inner soul in turmoil and his heart ashamed.

Without warning, and with a sudden jolt, a great wall of water smashed into the racing car. The speedometer fell to zero as both car and driver were thrown furiously side to side in the raging water.

Garrett knew instantly that a flash flood, caused by thirty-five inches of water in three days, had crashed down on him and his helpless automobile, now pitching and rocking in a tempest of wind, rain and flooding waters. Exhausted and despairing, Garrett struggled to open the door. He pounded on the windshield and the side windows. He cried for help. There was no escape. The windows and doors were sealed shut.

The words of Bill Mason raced through his mind:

"We all must face eternity someday, whether we want to or not."

"What did we do with Jesus?"

Suddenly, the car careened, with great force, into the depths of the ocean below.

MARK 8:36
"For what doth it profit a man if he gain the whole world and lose his own soul."

ROMANS 6:23
"For the wages of sin is death, but the gift of God is eternal life through Christ Jesus our Lord."

ISAIAH 55:7
"Let the wicked forsake his way, and the unrighteous man his thoughts, and let him return unto the Lord, for He will abundantly pardon."

JOHN 3:16
"For God so loved the world, that He gave his only begotten Son, that whoever believes in Him should not perish, but have everlasting life."

HEBREWS 9:27
"For it is appointed unto men once to die, but after this the judgment."

SIGNS IN THE EARTH AND HEAVENS

LUKE 21:25-28

"AND THERE WILL BE SIGNS IN THE SUN, IN THE
MOON, AND IN THE STARS; AND ON THE EARTH
DISTRESS OF NATIONS, WITH PERPLEXITY, THE
SEA AND THE WAVES ROARING;
MEN'S HEARTS FAILING THEM FROM FEAR AND
THE EXPECTATION OF THOSE THINGS WHICH ARE
COMING UPON THE EARTH, FOR THE POWERS OF
THE HEAVENS WILL BE SHAKEN.

THEN THEY WILL SEE THE SON OF MAN COMING
IN A CLOUD WITH POWER AND GREAT GLORY.

NOW WHEN THESE THINGS BEGIN TO HAPPEN,
LOOK UP AND LIFT UP YOUR HEADS, BECAUSE
YOUR REDEMPTION DRAWS NEAR."

K imberly was excited. This was the final year in her organ studies at the University of Oklahoma; she was studying with the famous organ teacher Mildred Andrews. Her four years at the university had been amazing: serving as soloist with the orchestra, winning national competitions, playing numerous recitals, and receiving prestigious awards and honors.

Today was her final lesson on the music she would perform for her graduate recital which was to take place in two weeks. She ran into the concert hall, gave Professor Andrews a cheery hello, and sat down at the organ

"And what shall we hear today?" queried Miss Andrews, as she was affectionately known around the school.

"How about the Bach Toccata in F Major?" Kimberly replied.

"That will be fine. Go ahead, but not too fast," replied her master teacher.

Kimberly began the Bach piece with much confidence. She had practiced hard and memorized well the thousands of notes in the Toccata. Her fingers and feet were always secure, clear and bright in style and tempo. In the middle of the second pedal cadenza, all was going well when suddenly the sound of the organ began to quickly disappear.

Puzzled, Kimberly's hands quickly came off the keys.

"Click." The sound completely died and the organ went off. At the same time, the auditorium stage lights went black, leaving student and teacher sitting stunned in total darkness.

"What happened?" Kimberly asked.

"I don't know," replied Miss Andrews in an irritated tone. "Perhaps we should call the facility manager. He always fixes these kinds of things quickly."

"You can use my cell phone," replied Kimberly. "Let me

turn it on for you." She tapped the screen. Nothing happened.

"Humm…it's not turning on! The battery was fully charged when I came in today," said Kimberly, looking dismayed.

"Why don't we use my office phone?" Miss Andrews asked. "Could you just help me down the stairs? It's so dark."

They made their way into the half-lit hallway and into the organ department office. Miss Andrews flipped on the light switch… no light. She picked up the phone….no dial tone.

Kimberly peered out of the office window. A crowd of students were gathering outside on the lawn, all with cellphones, disturbed looks and frantic hand movements.

"Let me go out and see what's happening," she said, as she ran out the door to the crowd gathering outside.

"What's going on? Does anybody know?" Kimberly asked her friend.

"No," replied Danny, a voice student who was Kimberly's good friend. "All of a sudden, all the lights went out in our classroom: all the computers, cellphones, and electronic equipment. We were listening to opera arias on CD and everything went dead, instantly, all at the same time!"

Kimberly looked puzzled.

"I think I'll go down to the sorority house. Maybe they'll have some word about what's happening. See you all later," Kimberly said as she ran across the lawn.

The Delta Gamma house was only two blocks from the music school and Kimberly made it there in record time. Running in the front door, she was met by a crowd of her sorority sisters gathered in the front hallway.

"What's going on," she said breathlessly. "Did you all lose any electricity?"

"Are you kidding!?" her friend Rita barked. "Everything in the house is dead: cellphones, lights, TV's, radios, computers, refrigerators, and everything else you can think of.

Even the generator is dead—same with you?"

"Yeah, that's why I'm here. I was playing the organ in the auditorium, and—bummer—everything in the place went dead...died...nada!"

The front door behind her suddenly flew open and her boyfriend, John Bruner, practically fell in the door.

"Is everything okay here?" he said as he grabbed Kimberly and held her tightly. "I just ran over from the Phi Delt house to see if you all were safe. On the way over, I saw cars stopped on the side of the road, blocking intersections and driveways, the engines dead, just like everything at the fraternity house. There were mobs of students in the streets, standing in clusters, waving their hands, running back and forth to their cars and houses, fiddling with their cell phones. The scene was absolutely mad!"

"Have any of you been outside in the last twenty minutes?"

"I have." replied Kimberly. "There were hundreds of students outside the music building and all the way over here to the sorority. Everybody seemed dazed!"

"Not only that," John said, "but my fraternity buddy, Jack, just drove in from Oklahoma City. He said the same thing was happening all around the city, and on the way down to Norman. Cars were lined up alongside the highways, trucks standing in the middle of roads and intersections, people wandering around frantically. I'm amazed he made it with that old clunker he has. He couldn't understand why his car was running when nobody else's was. This is absolutely insane!"

Kimberly's sorority sister, Marla, who had been listening to the conversation walked up to Kimberly and John. Marla was a double major in Science and Engineering. She was a bit of a "nerd' everyone thought, but she was well-liked and known for her brilliance.

"John, did you say that all the cars were stopped along

the road except for your friend's old clunker?"

"Yes, that's what I said," John replied. "So strange!"

"Not really," Marla said, as she stepped in closer to the conversation. "All new cars are filled with computers and very old ones are not. If cellphones, lights and computers aren't working, wouldn't you think new, computerized cars wouldn't work either? It seems to me that maybe the whole electrical grid, including electricity, electronics, computers, and the like, have all been shut down. And if that's the case, what about airplanes, control towers, security infrastructures, gas stations, restaurants, and..."

"Wait," John interrupted. "My friend who drove from Oklahoma City said he saw several pillars of smoke off to the south, and to the west...big billows of black and grey smoke!"

"Planes. Crashed." Marla said intensely.

"You think about it," she continued, "most of modern life is built on electricity and electronics."

She paused. "There's only one explanation I can think of that would take out so many things. I don't know how widespread this all is, but if it's what I think may have happened, we are in real trouble...I mean catastrophic trouble."

"What's that, Marla?" Kimberly asked, with wide eyes.

Marla responded gravely; by now the crowd had grown to over one hundred girls, who hung on every word:

"There's something called an EMP, an electromagnetic pulse. It's a nuclear detonation that takes place at least twenty-five miles above the earth. If a terrorist group would explode these nuclear devices, let's say, over the middle of the country, it could instantaneously knock out *all* of the continental United States. All electric and electronic infrastructures would be taken down in seconds. Even many generators couldn't withstand it. There would be *no* means of communication, no phone, no internet, no transportation, no food and no way to transport it.

"Banks would lose all electronic records. No heat or air conditioning in homes and buildings—and that's just the beginning."

"Yikes, you guys," Marla exclaimed, looking at her wide-eyed audience. "This is catastrophic. And we're not talking about just weeks, or months, to get it fixed. We could be talking about a year or more!"

She looked around the room. The girls seemed terrified, and now the housemother had come in to listen.

"I want to call my family," cried Didi from the back of the room. "Can't I do that? I'm so scared!"

"That's just it," Marla continued. "Can you call you your family now? Can they call you? They're probably worried to death about us all. There's no way to get word to anybody! Can you drive your car, or do your homework with no computer? We don't have any lights in the sorority house, no way to cook food, and in a few days, we'll be completely *out* of food....and there will be no way for it to be transported in. I'm sure that in a few hours, when everybody finds out what's happened, all the stores and restaurants will be cleaned out of everything! And then what?"

"What can we do?" asked John.

"I have no idea," said Marla. "We just have to wait. How long, I don't know."

A knock at the sorority house door interrupted the intense conversation. Everyone watched as a young man in jeans and tee shirt asked breathlessly if he could come in. The housemother, looking worried, quickly opened the door.

"Hello, ma'am, and everybody," he said, turning to the crowd in the hallway. "My name is Bobby Bowan. I'm from the administration office and I was asked to contact as many campus organizations as I can. As you can see, I'm running from one place to another because there's no transportation...I'm sorry to be so out of breath, but I must be quick!"

Everyone stared, wide-eyed.

"A friend of the university vice-president is a ham operator. That's the only way to get any news, it seems. He was able to make a contact at the Pentagon, and we've been attacked by terrorists with what they believe is an EMP explosion. The same is true for Germany and Great Britain."

"Just as I thought," Marla muttered to herself.

"All infrastructure in the country is down…critical electrical grids are down. Their information is stark because of no communication systems, but it seems cities are in chaos. They've warned that it will be six months, if not longer, as no one is able to do anything. It's severe crisis mode. Nobody can help. I'm sorry, but I have to keep going."

The door slammed behind him.

"Oh, lord," somebody cried, "please help us!" Others dissolved in tears, crumbling to the floor in desperation.

Marla looked disgusted and angry.

"The government has known for a long time that a terrorist attack like this could happen, but they've done nothing to prepare for it and nothing to warn the American people! It's a shame! Nuclear scientists have been warning for years about the catastrophic danger of such an event….. It will send the entire country back to the eighteenth century. Our whole life is built high-tech, and now it's fried!"

"How did you learn about this, Marla?" the housemother asked with obvious alarm. "I'm sure nobody on campus knows as much as you do about what's happened."

"I only know about it because of my science class. We discussed it at length last semester and I did some additional research. Everybody said it would never happen. Now it's happened!"

"With 25,000 mouths to feed on this campus—and with no cars, no phones, and no communication—you can imagine everybody's going to be desperate. And good luck if anyone gets sick. The hospitals will be without oxygen, electricity, refrigeration for meds, and no running water!"

The room was silent.

It was around five o'clock p.m. and the afternoon shadows were beginning to cover the house. Soon it would be dark. What would they do for lighting? How would they cook the food for over one hundred girls? What would the coming days bring? These questions and more passed between the girls standing in the front hallway, each looking lost and terrified.

Kimberly was especially solemn. She turned to John.

"Please excuse me," she said. "I'm going over to the chapel before it gets dark. This is so serious."

"I understand," he responded.

Kimberly left the house and headed a block down the street to a place she loved so much. It was a small chapel where she had spent much time during her college years, praying for guidance and for the salvation of her fellow students and sorority sisters. As she walked, she passed the hundreds of cars, groups of confused students, and myriads of others who had come out of buildings and houses looking mystified and afraid.

She entered the chapel and was surprised to find no one but herself inside. In a way, she was glad to be alone. She was devoted to Jesus, and she just wanted to pray. She sat down in her favorite pew near the front of the chapel and looked at the cross on the front wall. She suddenly remembered a verse that she had heard many times, but now had more meaning than ever:

"IN THE LAST DAYS, THERE SHALL BE PERILOUS TIMES."

Yes, she knew and had thought a lot about the last days, the period before Christ returned for all believers, and the world would be changed forever. She thought about the Bible texts which warned of apocalyptic events that would take place during this time, and wondered if what was happening now might be a part of those end time catastrophes:

signs in the earth and heavens, earthquakes, wars and rumors of wars, famines, pestilence, floods, the roaring of the seas and oceans, violence and even terrorism. It seemed to her that all these things were now taking place, at the same time, and things were more serious than ever

She also realized this would seriously alter her plans for the future; no final recital, no practicing, and without that, no graduation.

She knelt at the chapel altar:

"Oh, Lord," she cried, "have mercy on me. Have mercy on my friends and sorority sisters, and all those who are lost and don't know you. I thank you that you are my savior, and that no matter what happens in this life, it is in your hands. Lord, please help me to encourage others and to tell them about Jesus. Thank you that you are our only hope in a dark world, and for your word that says, 'You are the way, the truth, and the life.' Oh, Jesus, I thank you for the hope and peace that you've given to me and those who know you, and the promise of eternal life. Please go with me now, I pray in Jesus name. Amen."

With God's peace, Kimberly walked slowly back to the sorority house...to face an unknown future.

Luke 21:26
"In the last days, men's hearts will fail them for fear and the expectation of those things which are coming on the earth, for the powers of the heavens will be shaken."

John 16:33
"And Jesus said,
'These things I have spoken to you, that in Me you may
have peace. In the world you will have tribulation:
but be of good cheer, I have overcome the world.'"

John 14:27
"Peace I leave with you, My peace I give unto you;
not as the world giveth, give I unto you. Let not your
heart be troubled, neither let it be afraid."

EARTHQUAKES

MATTHEW 24:7

*"FOR IN THE LAST DAYS, THERE WILL BE FAMINES,
PESTILENCES, AND EARTHQUAKES
IN VARIOUS PLACES
ALL THESE ARE THE BEGINNINGS OF SORROWS."*

Matthew 24:37
*"FOR AS IT WAS IN THE DAYS OF NOAH,
SO IT WILL BE AT THE COMING OF THE SON OF
MAN. FOR IN THE DAYS BEFORE THE FLOOD,
PEOPLE WERE EATING AND DRINKING, MARRYING
AND GIVING IN MARRIAGE, UP TO THE DAY NOAH
ENTERED THE ARK, AND THEY KNEW NOTHING
ABOUT WHAT WOULD HAPPEN UNTIL THE FLOOD
CAME AND TOOK THEM ALL AWAY. THAT IS HOW
IT WILL BE AT THE COMING OF THE SON OF MAN,
'THEREFORE BE READY, FOR YOU KNOW NOT WHAT
DAY YOUR LORD WILL COME.'"*

B en said goodbye to his wife and three children, and boarded the plane to Los Angeles. He was glad to be able to relax in one of the comfortable seats of his private Lear jet, and looked forward to a weekend with friends and a new girlfriend he had met several months earlier. He was receiving the most prestigious award from the World Athletic Association, and although he had been blessed with so many honors in the past, this was a special one.

He loved being with his three good friends, too, who would meet him at the airport along with Laura, his new "playmate." The four had been friends for years, and although not as famous as Ben, they were filthy rich and always ready for a party. They could also keep a secret, Ben thought, and since they had affairs, too, they always protected Ben from leaks to his family and the media.

Jim, Luke, and Don met Ben at the gate and the four friends walked together to meet Laura. They all noticed her at once as they approached the arrival hall: a beautiful slender blond, adorned in spike heels and a red slinky dress with dangling earnings.

"That has to be Laura," Jim said to Ben. "She looks like your type!"

"Yeah, she's pretty hot, don't you think?" Ben added. "Tell me I don't have good taste!"

They all agreed as they followed Ben to meet his new friend. It was a bit awkward at first, but Ben kissed her on the cheek and then introduced each one to Laura.

Having retrieved all the baggage, they jumped into the waiting limousine for their ride to the St. Lorenz Hotel, one of the most elegant in L.A. Since it was late afternoon, they decided to meet later for dinner in Ben's suite.

With several hours between their arrival and dinner, Jim,

Luke and Don all went down to the casino to play a few slots and pick up some dates for the evening. They arrived at Ben's suite around seven o'clock. With an enormous dinner served in the room and plentiful drinks, the evening quickly evolved into a full-blown orgy.

Ben really enjoyed being with Laura again, and the two sneaked off to Ben's room around midnight. The suite finally fell silent around three o'clock, and no one awakened until late the next morning.

Ben ordered breakfast for Laura and himself around eleven thirty. They both sat quietly, Ben reading the newspaper, with his picture on the front, and Laura, slowly sipping her coffee.

"Does your wife know about me, Ben?" Laura asked, as she pulled the paper away from his face.

"No, she knows nothing about you or anyone else," Ben replied. "She doesn't like to travel, so our relationship stays close to home."

He looked back at Laura in frustration.

"You already asked me that in our last meeting," he said irritably. "Our two worlds, yours and mine, must stay separate. It would be very bad for my career, my sponsorships, and my reputation for any of this to get out. Do you understand that?"

"Reputation s...t, what about me?" she fumed back. "Am I just a 'one-nighter,' or do you have them all over the country? The first time we were together, you said you loved me. Isn't that true?"

"Of course, it's true, but it takes time to build a relationship. We've only been together once," he said.

She knew he was lying, but what could she do? He was so famous and exciting, and for now, he was a high-class catch.

Ben returned to hiding behind his newspaper. In between the written lines, he thought about his other affairs. He always said the same thing to all the girls: that he loved them and they would always be together. He loved his wife, too, he thought, but he needed someone and something more. He had worked hard for his fame and fortune and deserved whatever he wanted. It was fun and exciting, and he loved the challenge.

Ben wasn't thrilled about going to the awards dinner that night. "Even though this was a special one, It was often pure drudgery, with all the giddy conversation and sickening adulation," he thought. The only positive part of being honored was the addition of more sponsorships, more money and more fame, and even that got old. He sometimes wondered if this was all life had to offer. Many people, including some of his athlete friends, had tried to share with him over the years about surrendering his life to Jesus Christ. They always insisted that only Jesus brought true meaning and fulfillment. However, Ben flatly rejected the Jesus talk. He already had everything that life could give, he thought. He had no time, and no need for such things.

One thing he really dreaded that day was telling Laura she couldn't go with him to the awards ceremony. He finally found the nerve to break the news late in the afternoon.

"Babe, I need to tell you something," said Ben, as he sat down with Laura on the couch, taking her hand in his. "I can't take you to the awards ceremony tonight. I'm so sorry. I know you've come a long way and were looking forward to it, but we really can't be seen in public like that. If the media got word of it, we would be on the front page of every paper in the country." He looked sheepish as he gave her the news, knowing she would be livid.

"What do you mean, Ben," she said, with fury in her voice. "I'm your date this weekend, right? And we do everything together, right?"

"Look, Laura, what is really important is that we're together alone this weekend, not that you go with me to some boring evening of speeches and senseless chatter. You won't miss anything."

"Miss anything!" she screamed. "I will miss you. That's why I'm here and I'm not going to stay in this room. I bought a dress and everything. You can't do this to me!" She stomped across the room.

Ben did not respond. He walked into the bedroom to shower and dress for dinner, leaving her in a rage in the suite sitting room. "How can she be so stupid," he thought, "to think I would show her off to the whole world when I have a wife and children at home?" Besides, he had built such a sterling reputation as being such a faithful family man.

Dressed in his pristinely tailored tuxedo, Ben kissed Laura goodbye and apologized again for having to leave her for the evening. Laura, who had been beating on his bedroom door and crying uncontrollably, turned away from his goodbye kiss.

"Do you take me for a fool, Mr. Ben?" she screamed as he left the room. "You won't hear the last of this!" she warned.

The dining hall was filled with celebrities from every field: movie stars, business tycoons, famous sports figures and leading politicians. Ben was escorted in to the room and taken to the head table where he was introduced to the other guests seated nearby.

"Pretty elite company," he thought, as he surveyed the other attendees. He was impressed with himself, he had to admit. Just like many of the other famous guests that evening, glittering in their elegant gowns and dashing evening clothes, Ben had assured his place in history as the most famous athlete in the world, and perhaps in history. No one had ever reached his achievements and notoriety. He had conquered the world on his own, in more ways than one, he mused.

The gourmet dinner was served with elegance. While waiting for dessert, Ben enjoyed the view from the seventieth floor dining room. The lights of L.A. glittered in all directions. "It is a beautiful city," he thought.

As he continued scanning the room, suddenly his eyes caught a sight that made his heart skip. It was Laura, dressed in a beautiful aqua gown, hair combed back and coiffed, standing in the back near the dining room entrance.

"What the h—- is she doing here!" Ben fumed. "I told her we could not be seen together!"

The room was filled with over five hundred guests, all enjoying the company of other elites and delicious gourmet food. Suddenly Laura, with eyes aflame, marched through the tables to the front. She approached the head table, greeting the other guests as she walked by. Stopping directly in front of Ben, she leaned over the table, slapping him in the face as hard as she could swing. "You bastard," she screamed. "You are an adulterer, a fake, a low-life and a disgrace to the world, your wife and your children!"

Ben was aghast. He tried to lean over the table and grab her arm. She pulled away and continued her shouting as she turned toward the audience.

"This man you are honoring tonight and calling a 'hero' has ruined my life, and the life of many others like me. He is living a debased life while you clap and adore him with your highest of honors!"

Her voice carried from the nearby podium microphone throughout the room and even into the hallways. Maître D's and servers stopped to stare at this strange and bizarre occurrence.

A security guard raced to the front. Shoving her aside, he led her screaming from the room. Her raging continued as she passed the tables on the way out.

The disbelieving crowd sat in stunned silence.

Ben was humiliated. In a few minutes, he would be called upon to receive his award and make an acceptance speech. He wanted to run away as fast as his legs would carry him, but he was stuck. There was no way out. He lowered his eyes to the table, waiting for the master of ceremonies to make his comments and introductions.

The silence of the room was broken by the emcee speaking in a clearly shaken tone of voice:

"Ladies and gentlemen, please excuse this embarrassing and uncalled for disruption. As you know, these things can happen in public gatherings, by troubled and mentally disturbed people. Please accept our apology."

The ceremony continued and the honorees were introduced with polite appreciation and applause. Finally the emcee turned to Ben:

"And now, ladies and gentlemen," the emcee announced proudly, "let's all welcome Mr. Benjamin Goods, our most distinguished and honored Person of the Year!"

The crowd, jumping to their feet, burst into spontaneous and uproarious applause. Ben stood and took his bows, humiliated, but still holding his head high. He moved to the microphone and with a shaking hand, placed his scribbled speech on the podium.

"Good evening, everyone," he said, his eyes combing the room, afraid of any other bizarre outbursts. "I want to thank you for honoring me with this most incredible award. I don't deserve it—but I will accept it!" The room laughed and applauded again.

"It is a…a great privilege to be….to be with you tonight," he continued, stumbling over his words, wandering how he was going to explain the preceding outburst. "Should I say anything? Or let it go?" he thought

The room was dead silent. Moments seemed like hours to Ben as he searched for the words to say.

Suddenly, from the back of the room, a sound of tinkling

glass caught the ear of both Ben and the attentive audience. "Is somebody hitting their glass with silverware? Or has something broken on a table?" Ben wondered. People scanned the room, quickly returning their attention to the speaker. Ben continued slowly, the listeners again silent.

"I would like to make a short explanation of..."

Again, an even louder sound of shattering glass now erupted from every corner of the dining room. Shocked and alarmed, the eyes of the audience darted in every direction. No one wanted to be the first to move.

Ben, the famous and honored speaker, was smitten with fright.

Abruptly, the sound of breaking glass, now joined by a thunderous roar, came closer and closer.

Ben's thoughts went wild. This couldn't be another 9/11, could it? Surely it can't be a plane.

Terrified, the crowded room broke into chaos. An elegant lady in beautiful white satin, seated at the head table, was the first to leave. Grabbing her husband, dressed in his most formal attire, she raced from the room toward the exit door. One by one, people threw back chairs and tables, fleeing in terror, for any way of escape. A famous movie star, dressed in red sequins and elaborate jewelry, shouted out to God for mercy, stumbling over others to reach the back exit. There were too many people to get through.

"It must be an earthquake," she screamed, shoving and crowding into other lines headed for a side door.

Suddenly, a deep, cracking sound thundered throughout the room. With screams and wailing from terror-stricken guests, the beautiful crystal chandeliers rocked back and forth wildly from the ceiling.

A man shouted from the back: "This exit is closed....the steps are buckling. Try another, try another!" He pointed to a forward opening.

Benjamin, still standing, was frozen with shock and

desperation.

He thought of his fame, his money, his honors...but no one cared anymore about him or his award.

He thought of his family...his children...his lovers...his lies...his secret sins.

He remembered his flat rejection of Jesus, for whom he had no time.

With self-loathing, he cringed. "I am a fool!"

But now, it was every man for himself.

Ben suddenly emerged from his stupor. He was the world's most famous athlete, with great strength. He would escape if he had to crush everyone in his path. He jumped over the head table, running over bodies, chairs, and tables.

Suddenly, with a deep rumbling sound as if the earth was giving way, the room went black. There were no more beautiful lights of L.A. in the distance—everything had turned to darkness. With a deafening roar, the building, seventy stories high, appeared to divide in the middle, casting the elite and honored crowd towards opposite sides of the room, through broken windows and glass. Others, including Benjamin Woods, fell into the chasm which had opened up in the middle, as though swallowed up by a bottomless pit. The building swayed as it cracked beneath its weight, like paper blown by a great wind.

All that was left was the screaming, the crying, the groaning of victims, the breaking of glass, the grinding of stone, and steel, the darkness and suffering.

Ben was no longer adored, no longer revered. He was hopeless, alone, eternally lost.

Luke 13:3
"Except ye repent, ye shall all likewise perish."

Proverbs 28:1
"He that covereth his sin shall not prosper; but whoso confesseth and forsaketh them shall have mercy."

Hebrews 9:27
"It is appointed unto man once to die, but after this the judgment."

Mark 8:36
"For what doth it profit a man, if he gain the whole world and lose his own soul."

PESTILENCE

MATTHEW 24:7

"IN THE LAST DAYS THERE WILL BE
FAMINES, PESTILENCE AND EARTHQUAKES
IN VARIOUS PLACES."

"**D**ad, would you go to church with mother and me this morning?" asked Blake, as she finished her usual Sunday breakfast of German pancakes and bacon. She always asked her dad to attend church with her, but he always had his usual excuses and would promise to go "sometime soon."

Today, however, she was going to be insistent.

"Please, Dad?" she pleaded.

"No, Blake," her dad responded. "You know I have a golf game with my buddies every Sunday. They would be disappointed if I didn't come."

"But, Dad," Blake responded, as she got up from the table and walked toward him. "I would be disappointed if you don't go! Who is the most important to you?"

"Honey, you know Marsha and you are more important than anyone to me," he stated emphatically.

Mark folded up his Sunday paper and continued as he faced her squarely.

"I work very hard during the week to support our family. I'm at the office eight hours every day, sometimes even longer. I just need to rest and relax during the weekend. It helps me get ready for another hard week. You understand that, don't you, honey?" he stated in a matter-of-fact tone.

"No, Dad, I don't understand," she said, as she sat down frustrated on the couch beside him. "It's only one hour a week, eleven to twelve on Sunday. It's a chance for us all to be together and worship God! Don't you care about that?"

"Well, you know, Blake, the golf game also begins at eleven on Sunday and I just can't do both."

Blake turned her face away, and then turned back in disgust.

"Dad, don't you care about God. Isn't a chance to worship

Him and learn more about the Bible important, too?"

Mark hesitated. He knew on the inside that he felt church and that "God stuff" was a waste of time. It was good maybe for old women and children, he thought, but not for him.

"Yes, of course I care about God," he answered, "but I can think about Him on the golf course—and maybe some other time we can go."

"Oh yeah, right!" Blake muttered to herself.

It made her heart sad, but it seemed like a futile conversation. She had tried so many times to persuade him.

"Okay, Dad," Blake said, as she walked away. "We'll see you later."

"Okay, honey," Mark responded. "Thanks for understanding."

Mark dressed for golf, and Blake and her mother left for church. It was a wonderful service, with beloved hymns and uplifting music by the choir. The sermon was especially meaningful to Blake. It was on Matthew 6:33: "Seek ye first the kingdom of God and all these things will be added unto you."

She wanted so much for her father to love God as she did. In her first year of high school while attending church with a friend, she had committed her life to Christ in the service. Since then, her life had been so different, even transformed. She wanted so much for her father to know Jesus in a personal way.

Mark and his friends had a very raucous and successful golf game. They all played well, but Mark was the best. He actually made thirteen pars, four birdies and only one bogey, when his ball went into the lake and he had to wade into the water to hit it out. Nevertheless, it was his best game ever. They all had a "great old time" celebrating in the club with drinks following the match.

On the way home from the club, Mark noticed a small red dot on his ankle which had begun itching terribly. "It must be a bite of some kind," he thought, "probably a mosquito. There are a lot of those around the water holes these days with all the rain." He also was feeling badly about his conversation with Blake that morning. Perhaps he just might give in the following Sunday and go with her and her mother to church. He wouldn't like it but he would do it—maybe.

The following day, the week began as usual. Mark went off to his office, Blake to school, and Marsha remained at home to do household chores. She had a bridge game that afternoon, too, which she looked forward to. During the week, the family didn't see much of each other in the evenings, as there were different activities, homework and various other social engagements.

On Wednesday night, however, the whole family gathered for dinner, a rare occasion. It was the usual mundane conversations: "How are you doing?" "How did your day go?" "What will you do tomorrow?" When a sudden strangeness came over Mark, who sat staring emptily into space. He seemed over-fatigued and complained of a nauseating headache and fever.

"Perhaps you should go lie down, Dad," Blake said in a worried voice.

"No, I think it'll go away soon, I hope," Mark responded, looking pale and weak. "Perhaps I should take some tylenol or something."

"I'll get some for you, honey," said Marsha, as she grabbed several pills from the kitchen cabinet.

As he reached out for the pills, both Marsha and Blake noticed his hand shaking, uncontrollably. He could hardly move his left hand to his mouth. Blake and her mother both tried to lift him up to lead him to the sofa. His legs were limp and wouldn't carry his weight.

He fell to the floor.

"Quick, Blake, call 911, something is terribly wrong," Marsha shouted. Blake, with trembling hands, dialed the number, explained the situation to the operator, and quickly hung up. She ran to her father, placed her arms around his shoulders and waited anxiously for the ambulance.

Blake and Marsha accompanied Mark to the hospital. With a flurry of activity, the emergency staff took over Mark's care from the ambulance. They all seemed compassionate and extremely competent. As they rolled him into the emergency room, Martha noticed that he seemed almost unconscious. Both she and Blake begged to stay with him, but were advised to go to a waiting room for the families.

Two, three, four hours passed with no word from the doctors. It seemed like an eternity for Blake and Marsha. After about four and a half hours, Dr. Kincaide, Director of Emergency Services, entered the room. A middle-aged, silver-haired man, he seemed kindly and compassionate.

He greeted them both, motioning for them to sit down. He could tell they were exhausted both mentally and physically.

"I'm sorry to have kept you waiting so long," be began. "It's apparent through the tests and MRI that your husband, and father, has come down with a very severe case of West Nile Virus."

He paused.

"I'm sure you've heard about this disease that's been blanketing the country in the last several months. A real plague, I would say. It's spread by mosquitoes and unfortunately, as yet, there is no treatment or vaccine for the virus."

He looked at both Blake and Marsha intently.

"To your knowledge, do you know if Mark has been around any standing water, lakes or ponds in the last several days?" he asked.

Blake dropped her head.

"He's been in his office every day this week, but..." she paused.

"He did play golf on Sunday and I know there are several lakes on the course" she replied. "Perhaps you can ask him—he would know."

Dr. Kincaide hesitated.

"I'm sorry, Blake, but we can't ask him. Your father is one of the few victims of West Nile who has come down with meningitis; a disease, as you may know, that affects the neurological system. He's now in a coma, but even if he comes out of it, he'll have paralysis of one or more limbs, and probably palsy."

"Oh, no!" Blake cried out. Her mother cried quietly and put her arm around Blake.

"How can this be?" Marsha said, as she stared disbelieving at the doctor. "He was just fine several hours ago?"

Dr. Kincaide waited, then answered in a compassionate tone.

"That's the way this disease works. It takes some days for the symptoms to appear. One out of every 150 people who are bitten by the mosquitoes have severe symptoms, and for some, it is fatal."

"Let me be honest," he continued. "His condition is life-threatening. We just can't know what will happen from here. We can only pray for a miracle."

The silence was tragic.

Blake, who had been standing near the doctor, fell into a nearby chair and cried with bitter tears. She remembered the words of her dad from Sunday:

"It's okay, Blake...I promise to go to church with you soon..."

PROVERBS 27:1
"Boast not thyself of tomorrow, for thou knowest not what a day may bring forth."

II CORINTHIANS 6:2
*"Behold, now is the accepted time, now is
the day of salvation!"*

MATTHEW 24:13
*"Therefore, you also be ready, for the Son of Man (Jesus)
is coming back at a time you do not expect."*

PERILOUS TIMES

2 TIMOTHY 3:1

*"BUT KNOW THIS, THAT IN THE LAST DAYS FIERCE
AND PERILOUS TIMES WILL COME."*

Nathan walked in the front door of his home of thirty years. His wife, Jinny, met him at the door and knew immediately that something was wrong.

"You look upset, Nathan," she said. "What's the matter?"

"You're not going to like it, Jinny," he said sadly. "I lost my job today. My boss called me in just as I was leaving to come home. He told me the once thriving business was going bankrupt and he had to let me go, along with ninety-five other employees. I couldn't believe my ears. Just like that," he said, as he snapped his fingers.

Shocked and dismayed, Jinny tried to give words of encouragement.

"I'm so sorry, honey," she said, placing her hand in his. "It certainly has nothing to do with you and your abilities. It's just happening everywhere with this terrible economy and other natural disasters. But you're so gifted at what you do. You'll find another job soon, I'm sure."

Jinny was, herself, shaken by the news. She was a person of deep faith and courage, but she also knew that with two teenage children and hefty monthly bills, it wasn't going to be easy.

Nathan shook his head as he sank down in his favorite armchair. It had all happened so suddenly. He was not mentally or emotionally prepared for such life-changing news. It was as though suddenly a mountain of debt, worry and uncertainty had been cast upon his mind and soul.

Jinny walked over to Nathan and laid her hand on his.

"Nathan, I am a great believer in God and the power of prayer. We will ask Him to help us—and I know He will. Just take one day at a time. We'll be okay."

Nathan nodded almost painfully.

The following day, Nathan began his job search. Hours

on the computer turned into days and months of long and discouraging research, phone calls, meetings and interviews. The unemployment lines in which he found himself many times sometimes numbered over a thousand people—each waiting, worrying and finally being asked to write a job application which turned into rejection.

Even worse for Nathan were the bills that kept coming relentlessly to the house. Their savings were now gone, and Nathan and Jinny had been forced to borrow money from both of their families. He hated doing that, and felt angry about having to do so. The children were placed on a strict budget: no movies, no new clothes, no outings with friends or even with the family. There was no money for non-essentials.

After months of futile searching and constant anxiety, Nathan was giving up. He had lost all hope, sense of pride, and self-esteem. He realized he now was just one of the awful numbers that he had read and heard about for years: twenty-four million without jobs; one in every six living in poverty; 25 percent living on food stamps; over 350,000 a month giving up and dropping out of the job market.

Jinny had pleaded with Nathan numerous times to get away from the computer, the seemingly dead-end job hunting and the mindless television watching.

"Why don't you get out of the house and do something positive," she said kindly to Nathan. "How about going over to the church and volunteering several hours a week? The church folks have been so kind during this difficult year, and maybe it will relieve some of your stress."

"Jinny is right," Nathan thought. Even though he had never attended church, still these people had been kinder than anyone to him and his family. Various church members had invited them often for dinner, helped around the house and yard, and took the girls out for entertainment and special weekends. Others called daily to see if there was anything they could do. "That is truly 'loving your neighbor,'" he thought.

"Okay, Jinny," he said sheepishly one day. "I'll volunteer at the church, but only a few hours a week."

Jinny was pleased and felt that even though times were desperate, her prayers were being answered. She couldn't wait to find out what might happen.

The next morning, Nathan showed up at the small but beautiful Redeemer Church, and started his menial but pleasant tasks. He was glad to clear his mind and talk to people who, he felt, sincerely cared. He was always greeted by cheery hellos, kind words and loving actions. He needed that special feeling of being appreciated by others. It somehow helped the terrible gnawing he had in the pit of his stomach. He felt he couldn't handle his depressed state much longer.

One Thursday afternoon, several weeks into his volunteer work, a kindly, gray-haired man was preparing one of the rooms for a Bible study that night.

"Can I help you?" said Nathan, as he peeked his head around the corner.

"Yes, of course you can," the man said smiling. "And by the way, my name is Gary Findlay, and I know you as Nathan Hart, Jinny's husband. I want to thank you for all the work you've been doing around the church lately. A helping hand is always appreciated."

Nathan smiled. "Well, it's good to be giving a helping hand where I am needed. It takes me away from my troubles."

"You know, Nathan," Gary replied. "Many folks in this town are having severe hardships and difficulties. These are perilous times and we all need encouragement. I'm just preparing the room for a Bible study here tonight. Would you like to come? It might give you a lift. It's at seven thirty if you can make it."

"I'll think about it," Nathan replied, "and thanks for the invitation."

On his drive home that afternoon, Nathan thought about

Mr. Findlay. There was a kindness and courageous spirit in this man—a lot like Jinny, he thought. He had never liked church or "church people" very much, but somehow these people were different. He felt a special presence and love coming from each one.

"Everything else I've tried this past year has failed," he told himself. "I'll try this Bible study once—but that's it."

At seven thirty, Nathan quietly edged into the back row of the Bible study room. He was a little late, and the study was just beginning, led, of course, by Gary Findlay who was just finishing his opening prayer.

"Lord, we pray that you will open our eyes tonight to your truth. Help us to feel your presence and to know you love us and have a special plan for our lives. In Jesus' name we pray. Amen."

The evening lesson was built on the Bible text from Jeremiah 29:11:

"FOR I KNOW THE PLANS I HAVE FOR YOU,' DECLARES THE LORD, 'PLANS TO PROSPER YOU AND NOT TO HARM YOU, PLANS TO GIVE YOU A HOPE AND A FUTURE."

"Wow, what a promise," Nathan thought as Mr. Findlay continued with the explanation of this powerful verse. "Surely this can't be a promise for me," thought Nathan as he listened intently. "I've never cared anything about God. Why would he love and care for me?"

At the end of the evening, everyone left the room, with only Nathan and Gary Findlay staying behind. Something in Nathan's spirit caused him to want to pour out his heart to this kind man. He was so depressed, and knew that he desperately needed help.

"That was a wonderful lesson tonight, Mr. Findlay," Nathan said

"Thank you," responded Mr. Findlay. "Please just call me Gary! I'm so glad you were here! Would you like to talk for a minute?"

"Yes, Gary, I would." Nathan said. "I guess I would like just to ask you why God would love me enough to make me a promise of having a plan for my life. I feel so unworthy, and I've never really been interested in spiritual things."

"Nathan," Gary responded, "God loves you and cares about every detail of your life. He is only waiting for you to come to Him and believe in His Son. It is only when you have a personal relationship with Christ that you can know Him and His ways. He wants to bless you, Nathan. He is just waiting for you to make that very important decision."

Nathan stared down at the floor. He could hardly keep the tears from filling his eyes.

"Gary, it looks like I have been brought to my knees this past year with no job and all the other difficulties I and my family have experienced. I don't know who I am anymore. I'm literally without hope. I've tried everything I can, but it isn't working. I truly feel I want to know this relationship with Christ you're talking about."

"Nathan, if that is what you really want," said Gary, "you can pray right now and ask Jesus to be the Lord of your life."

"I would like that," Nathan responded.

The two men knelt together and prayed for the Lord to be present with them.

Nathan, in his own words, cried out to God:

"Jesus, I have failed in so many ways, but tonight I feel your great love. I want to know your peace and forgiveness. Please come into my heart and make me a new person. I thank you, in Jesus' name, amen."

Gary was very moved by such a sincere and earnest prayer. He put his hand on Nathan's shoulder.

"Nathan," Gary said, "the Bible says that anyone who is in Christ is a new creature, old things are passed away, behold all things are become new. You have just given your life to Christ and He now lives within you. He has promised to lead you and be a light unto your path, and most of all, to give you peace and hope. It's important now that you read and study God's word, pray, and find a good church where you will have fellowship with other believers. Hopefully, I'll see you Sunday in worship here with Jinny. I know she has prayed and waited a long time for you to join her!"

"Thank you, Gary," Nathan responded with great emotion. "Even now, I feel that peace you just talked about—a load has been lifted from my life. Even though I still don't have a job, yet, my heart is somehow filled with hope."

Gary responded kindly. "The Bible explains that peace, Nathan. Jesus said, 'In the world you shall have tribulation, but be of good cheer, I have overcome the world.'"

As Nathan left the church that night, he felt like a new man. He couldn't wait to get home and tell Jinny—and that he would be joining her in church on Sunday!

Jinny was waiting at the door when Nathan drove into the driveway. He had called her on the way home and told her something wonderful had happened to him. She greeted him with open arms.

"I gave my life to Jesus, Jinny," he said. "I'm going to be a new man."

Her eyes filled with tears. She knew her prayers were answered, and she wondered what would happen next.

The coming Sunday morning, Nathan, Jinny and the two girls joined together for the first time in worship. It was one of the most special days Jinny could ever remember. The presence of God was very real in the service, and the sermon on "God's Peace," it seemed to Jinny, was so appropriate for their whole family.

Following the service, many people in the congregation introduced themselves to Nathan and thanked him for his months of volunteer work. After most everyone had left, Nathan and the family were leaving the sanctuary, when a distinguished man approached Nathan and introduced himself. Jinny couldn't remember seeing him before in the services but thought, perhaps, he was a new member.

"Hello, Nathan," said Henry Winston, who held out his hand in greeting. "My name is Mr. Winston, and I'm a visitor at the services this morning as a friend of the minister. He was telling me before the service about your volunteer work here at the church, and that you were looking for a job in the healthcare business. I'm the director of the hospital here in Camden, and I've been searching for a person to do marketing at the hospital. Our marketing director moved out of town several months ago, and I've heard that marketing is your field."

"Yes, sir, that's true," Nathan stammered, almost unable to get the words out. "I was Director of Marketing and Public Relations at a large health care provider here in town for over twenty-two years."

"Why don't you come and see me in the morning, Nathan," replied Mr. Winston. "Perhaps something can be worked out," he said with a smile.

Nathan could hardly breathe as he and the family got into the car. His mind was spinning with so many new dreams and hopes, and especially that wonderful peace that had come over him after he prayed at the Bible study that week. He thought of the sermon and the words of the wonderful hymn they had just sung at the end of the service:

"Peace, perfect peace
In this dark world of sin
The blood of Jesus whispers peace within.

Peace, perfect peace,
Our future all unknown,
Jesus we know
And He is on the throne."

The next morning, at ten o'clock, Nathan made his way to the hospital, the largest in the city, where he was directed to the office of Henry Winston. Nathan had emailed his resume to Mr. Winston the night before so he would be prepared for the meeting the next day. He was greeted with a hearty welcome, and the two sat down for over an hour of spirited conversation about everything from the job position, to the church, to world affairs, to the best restaurants in town. As Nathan thought during their time together, they really "hit it off."

Toward the end of the meeting, Mr. Winston became more serious.

"Nathan," he said, "I am a firm believer in Jesus Christ. I believe that when our lives belong to Him that He guides us in every area of life, and that when we pray, he answers our prayers. He has proven that to me many times in my life. I believe that our meeting yesterday, and my coming to that church as a guest, was not just a coincidence."

He paused, and then continued, looking intently into Nathan's eyes:

"I've been praying for someone to fill this position, and as I read your resume last night and have talked with you this morning, I believe you are the perfect person for the job. If you are interested, I would like to offer you the Director of Marketing and Public Relations position—starting as early as tomorrow!"

Nathan could hardly bring himself to speak. His heart was beating faster than he had ever remembered. He thought of the Bible study last week and his decision to make Christ the Lord of his life. He recalled the powerful text: "I KNOW THE PLANS I HAVE FOR YOU, DECLARES THE LORD; PLANS TO PROSPER YOU AND NOT TO HARM YOU; PLANS TO GIVE YOU A HOPE AND A FUTURE."

"Mr. Winston, I thank you and I thank God," Nathan stated firmly.

"Yes, I accept your offer—and I will begin tomorrow!"

PSALM 37:4,5
"Commit your way to the Lord, trust also in Him,
and He shall bring it to pass."

MATTHEW 6:33
"Seek ye first the kingdom of God and His righteousness
and all these things shall be added unto you."

PHILIPPIANS 4: 6
"Don't be anxious for anything, but in everything by prayer
and supplication, with thanksgiving, let your requests
be made known to God, and the peace of God,
which surpasses all understanding, will guard your hearts
and minds through Christ Jesus."

FAMINES

MATTHEW 24:7

"IN THE LAST DAYS, THERE SHALL BE FAMINES."

"I don't know how much longer we can go on, Lisa," Randall said, as he sat down for breakfast on a hot and dry Monday morning. As always, he had been out in the fields since dawn, looking over his burned and wilted crops. There had been no rain for months, and not much hope for the future.

"I don't know what to do, either, Randall," Lisa responded with a weary, sleepless expression. Usually a positive and hopeful person, Lisa could not keep her feelings of despair secret any longer. She couldn't bear to contemplate the loss of a year's work, and the effect it would have on the whole family. Since the spring planting, Randall, Lisa and their son, Stephen, had nurtured the soil for this year's income. Now, there would be no income, and bills had to be paid.

"You know, Lisa," Randall said. "I read in the paper this morning that this is one of the worst droughts in history, with over half of the country experiencing severe and lasting conditions. Of course, they don't have to tell us that! We already know because we're living it. But it's even more frightening to see it in print! People are at a loss to know what to do, including me!"

Lisa's eyes filled with tears.

"I'm so sorry, honey," she said in a quiet voice. "I've tried to help with a part-time job at the drug store, but it just isn't enough. I feel terrible about it."

"Don't feel it's your fault, Lisa. It's a combination of everything." Randall said, with eyes downward. "Losing 40 percent of our savings three years ago didn't help either. That horrible economic meltdown nearly wiped us out—we're running on an empty tank," he added, with hurt and sarcasm.

"It seems like the whole world is coming apart," Randall continued, staring blankly out at the parched fields. "You can't live without hope or money, and I'm not going on food stamps!"

There was a long silence in the room.

"Well, we have to try and keep our spirits up," Randall said, trying to encourage Lisa and himself. "Maybe something good will happen. I think Sammy and I will go out on the porch for a while. Maybe he'll have an idea," Randall stated flatly, trying to keep the mood from deteriorating any further.

Sammy was the family dog; a beautiful golden labrador retriever, who had a special kinship with Randall and followed him everywhere. Sammy's eyes were penetrating and compassionate. They had brought encouragement to his master so often and especially in this devastating time. Randall always felt Sammy understood everything, and that helped him to cope.

Together they sat down on the front porch, Randall on the swing, with Sammy at his feet. In good times, the swing was a place of total relaxation, looking over the land that he loved, and watching the clouds meander by as they cast their shadows on the tall, slender stalks of corn. He loved gazing at the Mississippi River as it rolled peacefully by on a warm and lazy day. The view of the fertile land brought energy into his soul, he thought. There was nothing more fulfilling than watching a tiny seed become a waving shaft of wheat, a stalk of corn, or a beautiful flower.

Now the ground was parched. Large cracks in the soil covered hundreds of acres of his once rich land. As far as he could see, there was no relief from this terrible blight that had wrecked his farm. Even his home was cracking at the foundations from the dry and shrinking soil. Big gaps and holes were forming under the house from the foundations settling in the heat. Doors, dead bolts and windows were difficult to open and close. Trees, plants, and flowers which had beautified the exterior were also victims of the deadly heat and famine. It reminded him of his soul, he thought, the barrenness of having nothing to live for, and the total loss of hope. He knew Lisa felt the same.

Randall looked over toward his neighbor's property. His dear friends, John and Terry Sullivan, were suffering, too. They owned over 150 head of cattle. With little food for the cows, the animals were bone thin with further dehydration from lack of water. With many days of over 100 degree temperatures, many of the cows were aborting their calves from "heat stress." He wanted to help his faithful friends so badly, but with only wilted crops and very little water himself, there was nothing he could do.

Even the nearby Mississippi was now literally drying up. The traffic on the river had dwindled to half of its normal activity. Sand bars usually found along the shore were now visible in the middle of the river with warning flags to barges and boats of low or no water.

Randall patted his beloved companion.

"We have to do something, Sammy," he said. Sammy looked up as if to understand his master's words.

"We're at the 'bottom of the barrel.' We've got to get help. Come on in, Sam, let's go talk to Lisa."

The two walked slowly into the house and found Lisa at the kitchen table. She was crying. Sammy walked over and put his head in her lap. The scene was too heartbreaking for Randall, as he went over and knelt by Lisa's chair.

"Maybe we could pray and ask for God's help, Lisa. We don't go to church very much, but surely God sees our suffering and wants to help us. I remember that verse I heard in Sunday school as a child. It went something like: 'Come unto me everybody who is burdened and carrying a heavy weight and I will give you rest.'"

Lisa shook her head in agreement and patted Sammy on the head. He stayed close.

The phone rang in the living room, and Randall got up

from his knees to answer the call.

"Hello, Randall Swanson speaking."

"Hello, Randall, this is Pastor Samson calling from the Covenant Church. I just thought I would give you a ring and see how you're doing. We've missed you at worship and many folks have asked about you."

"Well, pastor, you probably know how hard things have been around here. We just haven't felt like coming .We're in pretty bad emotional straits, I have to admit," Randall said sadly. "Could you come out and see us—we could really use your help."

"Of course," Pastor Samson replied enthusiastically. "I was just thinking I would like to come and visit. What about tomorrow evening about seven? Would that be okay?"

"Sure, pastor," said Randall, with a more hopeful tone. "We look forward to seeing you then."

"Okay, I'll be there."

Randall hung up the phone. "Amazing," he thought, "that the pastor whom we have not seen in months would call at this moment." He went to tell Lisa. Sammy still had his head in her lap and she was patting his forehead.

Pastor Samson arrived at the house the next evening right on time. Randall and Lisa met him at the door and welcomed him into the living room.

"Won't you sit down, Pastor?" Lisa asked. "How about some tea or coffee?"

"No thanks, Lisa," the pastor responded. "I won't be staying long—just wanted to chat for a few minutes."

Sammy joined the conversation at the base of Randall's chair as the three talked about the difficulties that were taking place in the world, and especially in their local community.

"I've had many families returning to the church this year," Pastor Samson said. "It seems that they have no place else to turn to but God, so they're coming to worship, and also attending some of the Bible studies. People have been surrendering their lives to Christ and truly finding new hope for living."

Pastor Samson continued with compassion. "What about you folks? Do you feel that you have a personal and vital faith in Jesus Christ?"

"Funny you would ask that, Pastor," Randall replied. "I was just telling Lisa before you called that I am sure God cares about us and our suffering. Surely if we pray, He will help us."

"May I ask you both a very important question?"

"Yes, of course," Randall responded.

"If you were to die tonight, do you believe that you would go to heaven?"

They both hesitated. Lisa responded first. "No, I guess I'm not sure—although I always hoped I would."

"I really don't know if I'd go to heaven or not," Randall answered thoughtfully.

"May I ask another question?"

"Yes."

"If you were to die tonight and stand before God, and he asked you, 'Why should I let you into my heaven,' what would you say?"

Randall and Lisa were silent, in deep thought.

"Well," Randall answered, "we've always been good people, tried to help others. I don't think we've really done anything bad, and we've both tried as hard as we can."

"I'm sure you have," Pastor responded. "May I share with you what the Bible says about that? First, it states in Romans 3:23 that, 'All have sinned and come short of the glory of God.'

"In other words, all of us have sinned and therefore we are in need of a savior. It also says in Ephesians 2:8 and 9: 'For by Grace are you saved, through faith, and that not of yourselves. It is the gift of God, not of works, lest any man should boast.'

"This means that we are not saved by how good we are, or how many things we do right, or how hard we try. Although these are all good things, they are *not* good enough to get us into heaven. We are saved only by faith in Jesus Christ, who died on the cross and took upon Himself our sins.

"I am sure you know the famous verse, John 3:16: 'For God so loved the world, that He gave His only begotten Son, Jesus Christ, that whoso believes in Him shall not perish but have everlasting life.'"

"I guess I never really understood that," Randall said. "I thought that if you were good enough, went to church and did the best you could, that would get you to heaven."

"What about you, Lisa?" the pastor asked.

"Well, I've just always tried to be and do good, but I see now I haven't really received this gift of salvation."

"All that is required," Pastor Samson continued, "is that you receive Christ as savior, as an act of your will. Would you like to do that tonight? We can pray together."

Randall remembered his words to Lisa, "Why don't we pray, surely God loves us and will help us." This was no coincidence that the pastor called and was there that night.

"Yes, we would like to do that, Pastor," Randall said.

Lisa agreed. "We have been so hopeless, Pastor. I know this is an answer to prayer."

"Then let's pray together," said Pastor Samson.

"Dear Lord, thank you for sending Jesus Christ to die for my sins.

Right now, I ask you to forgive my sins and to come into my heart as Lord and Savior.

I surrender my life to you that I can live as the special creation that you intended me to be.

In Jesus' name I pray.

Amen."

Randall and Lisa repeated the words of the prayer together. The moment was a sacred one.

They looked into the eyes of Pastor Samson. He could see the sense of relief and peace which was now evident in their spirit and expression.

"This is the most important decision you will ever make," Pastor Samson exclaimed with rejoicing in his voice. "Whatever you may have to face in the coming days, you can be sure that Jesus lives in you and will give you strength and hope. Christ, himself, is your hope, not your circumstances. He has promised to take care of you when you belong to Him. You can trust him!"

They nodded with new confidence and even joy! Sammy was at their side.

Tomorrow would be a *new* day.

Very early the next morning, before dawn, Randall and Lisa were awakened by a great clap of thunder. The patter of a gentle rain could be heard against the windows, feeding the thirsty land, the flowers, the cattle, and the hearts of two people now at peace with God. The rain continued throughout the day, and the following day, and the day after…

Isaiah 44:
"FOR I WILL POUR WATER ON HIM THAT IS THIRSY
AND
FLOODS UPON THE DRY GROUND."

Psalm 107: 9
"FOR HE SATISFIES THE THIRSTY SOUL AND FILLS
THE HUNGRY SOUL WITH GOOD THINGS."

John 7:37
"JESUS STOOD AND CRIED OUT, SAYING,
IF ANYONE THIRSTS, LET HIM COME TO ME

AND DRINK.
HE WHO BELIEVES IN ME, AS THE SCRIPTURE
HAS SAID, OUT OF HIS HEART WILL FLOW RIVERS
OF LIVING WATER."

IN THE TWINKLING
OF AN EYE

I CORINTHIANS 15:51,52

"BEHOLD, I TELL YOU A MYSTERY; WE SHALL NOT
ALL SLEEP, BUT WE SHALL ALL BE CHANGED
IN A MOMENT, IN THE TWINKLING OF AN EYE,
AT THE LAST TRUMPET. FOR THE TRUMPET
WILL SOUND, AND THE DEAD WILL BE RAISED
INCORRUPTIBLE, AND WE SHALL BE CHANGED."

MATTHEW 24:39-42
"SO ALSO WILL THE COMING OF THE SON OF MAN BE.
THEN TWO MEN WILL BE IN THE FIELD; ONE WILL
BE TAKEN AND THE OTHER LEFT.
TWO WOMEN WILL BE GRINDING AT THE MILL;
ONE WILL BE TAKEN AND THE OTHER LEFT.

WATCH THEREFORE, FOR YOU DO NOT KNOW WHAT
HOUR YOUR LORD IS COMING
THEREFORE YOU ALSO BE READY, FOR THE SON OF
MAN IS COMING AT AN HOUR YOU DO NOT EXPECT

The girls had spent almost a month planning their summer vacation. Since high school, Mary, Natalie, Joanie and Meg had been the closest of friends. After graduation, they had all gone about their separate lives, but each summer came together to spend a month traveling to a favorite destination. It was something they all looked forward to each year.

Following high school, both Natalie and Mary had stayed in Cincinnati and had found jobs in the fashion industry. Joanie had moved to Lexington, Kentucky and was teaching French, while Meg was living in Chicago working at the Chicago Board of Trade.

This summer, they had decided to go to Asheville, N.C., visiting the surrounding area, and then traveling through the Blue Ridge Mountains, stopping at scenic towns and national parks along the way. Meg, who was especially good at details, was the route and lodging "manager," while Joanie took care of food and drinks along the way. Natalie would be driving her snazzy new car and Mary would handle the expenses and money.

On July 1, the friends met in Cincinnati, staying a day at Natalie's condo and then heading off on July 2nd. They were hoping to spend July 4 in Asheville, watching the firework displays and visiting the famous Biltmore Estate. Their time traveling in the car was as important as their destinations. They loved catching up with each other, talking about their boyfriends, learning about each other's activities during the past year, and sharing about thoughts and ideas on different subjects.

The friends had not really changed too much since high school. For the most part, they looked the same, except that Meg had frosted hair rather than her beautiful golden blond hair, and Mary had completely chopped her hair off, making her look like a tomboy. Joanie had lost a lot of weight and had turned out to be a real beauty. They all had different personalities but seemed to complement each other, and over the years had remained extremely close, even though miles apart.

It was Natalie that had changed the most. They all noticed it immediately when they came together on July 1. In high school and the two years following, she had been a rather quiet and moody person. She had been brought up in a broken home; her father had run off with another woman, forcing her mother to work for a meager living by working over twelve hours a day and coming home grumpy every night. Natalie had to take the responsibility of meals, cleaning the house, and paying the bills. Often, she was in a foul mood and let everybody know about it. She loved her friends, however, but wasn't always as kind to them as they expected her to be. Now something was different.

After spending a few hours in the car, Joanie finally got the nerve to ask Natalie what had happened that had changed her so much. Natalie seemed to be thrilled to tell her story.

"I'd love to tell you all about it, but are you sure you want to hear all this?" Natalie asked.

"Sure, Nat," Joanie said. "We've got plenty of time to hear every detail!"

"Yeah!" Meg chimed in. "We've got four weeks," she laughed. "That ought to be enough!"

Everybody agreed.

Natalie, who wasn't driving at the time, smiled and started her story with great delight.

"Well," she said, "during this past year, Jill, a new friend of mine from work, invited me to a Bible study at her church. I wasn't crazy about it at first, but to please her, I came along. To my great surprise, it was a fantastic experience and I just loved the people I met there. They all seemed to be so happy and upbeat—and 'with it!' You know, I thought at a Bible study there just might be a bunch of duds, but it wasn't like that at all."

"Anyway, I kept on going for several weeks. The third week, a young guy was asked to get up and talk about his personal faith in Christ and what it had meant in his life. He was so handsome and well-spoken, and what he said was just amazing. It really made me sit up and listen," she added enthusiastically.

"Are you bored yet?" Nat said, looking around.

"No, no, keep going!" they all chimed in.

"Okay, but tell me if you want me to stop." Nat answered.

"We told you we've got almost a month," Meg laughed.

"Well, the Bible lesson that night was on John 3 when Nicodemas—I guess I am pronouncing his name right—who was a religious leader of his day, came to Jesus and asked him how he could do all His miracles. Jesus just answered him and said that 'he must be born again.' Nicodemas didn't know what that meant, and I didn't either." Nat paused.

"What Jesus meant was that you are born of the flesh when you come into this world, but to know God, you must be born by the spirit. Do you all understand that?" Nat asked.

"Sort of," Meg replied.

"It means," Nat continued, "that the only way to enter the kingdom of God is to be born again by God's spirit. That happens by asking Christ to forgive your sins and come into your life."

She continued:

"So anyway, the Bible study leader asked if anyone there would like to make a commitment to Jesus Christ and be 'born again.' I didn't have to think about that long. I really wanted to have the joy and peace that the people at that meeting seemed to have. They were different, and I mean, 'really good' different. You all know I've had a pretty hard past with my father leaving my mother and all the unhappiness that went along with it."

"So what did you do?" Joanie asked with keen interest.

"I just prayed along with the leader and asked Jesus to come into my heart and make me a new person. And you know what, He did—and I *am* a new person!" she exclaimed.

"YEA!" Meg declared, and they all clapped.

"I think we all agree that you're really different!" Joanie said. "You just seem to have a special glow—a special presence, I guess you would say. And you're not an old grump anymore!"

They all laughed hysterically.

"Just one more thing, guys," Nat added, in a serious tone.

"I want you all to know Jesus, too. It's the most important decision you'll ever make. And Jesus is coming back someday soon. You're my best friends—I want you to be ready for His coming!"

"That's, okay, Nat," Joanie said. "We have plenty of time to talk about it!"

They had been on the road for over five hours that first day, each telling their own stories and sharing in experiences and hilarious laughter. Joanie was sitting in the front seat giving road directions along with the "GPS lady" to Natalie, who had now taken over the driving. The scenery was beautiful along the route with the rolling hills, beautiful trees and countryside. Everyone seemed to be taking in the beauty of the moment, and resting for a bit until the next stop.

Suddenly, without warning, the car swerved abruptly to the right as if completely out of control. Everyone screamed and Joanie grabbed the steering wheel in an automatic reflex. As she looked toward the driver's seat, in the same instant, like the blinking of an eye, Natalie was not there. Joanie shouted to the other two girls and tried to find the brake with her left foot.

"Natalie!" she screamed, trying to move over into the driver's seat herself.

"Where is Natalie!?" she screamed. "You guys, where is

94

Natalie—is she in the backseat?!"

The car was skidding along the side of the road now. Joanie slammed on the brake, throwing the two girls in the back into the front dashboard.

"Oh, my God!" Joanie screamed again. Meg and Mary were stunned. The car had suddenly careened into the deep ditch beside the highway, as the speedometer fell from seventy miles per hour to zero in seconds.

"Meg, Mary!' Joanie screamed again. "Are you okay—where is Natalie? We weren't paying attention, where is Natalie!?"

Joanie had only been paying attention to the brake, the steering wheel, and the fact that Nat was gone, and Meg and Mary were badly hurt. She hadn't had time to actually look at the highway itself and the other cars.

She lifted her head and saw a terrifying scene.

Cars and trucks were scattered all along the road, some badly damaged, others not. People had begun to jump out of their cars, shouting, running from one place to another, screaming for help and looking for people they couldn't find.

All in a matter of seconds it seemed, the world was coming to an end. Where was Natalie, what had happened to all these cars, and why were so many people running back and forth in panic?

Joanie tried to give attention to Meg and Mary. Meg didn't seem to be badly hurt, but Mary was groaning in agony.

A man was approaching the car. He was in a frenzy, wiping his forehead.

He banged on the window. Joanie was afraid to open it.

He shouted as loud as he could: "Have you seen my wife? She has red hair, she was driving the car—all of a sudden she was gone. The car drove off the road. I'm lucky to be alive. Where is my wife?" he shouted again.

Joanie shook her head no. The man ran to the next car. Other people, some badly injured, were also running along the road, stopping at other crashed or empty cars.

"What's happening?" Meg cried. "Are we in hell? Mary's in bad shape. We must call 911."

Joanie pulled out her cell phone as Meg tried to comfort Mary.

"We're calling for help," she told Mary. "Try to stay calm."

Joanie got only busy signals as she called the 911 number. No one was answering. She tried again and again.

Finally, a voice answered on the other end.

"911, can we help you?"

"Hello, hello!" Joanie said in a trembling voice. "We have an emergency here. Can you help us?"

"You and everybody else!" said the lady on the other end. "We have a nationwide emergency here—hundreds of calls are on hold. Everyone is asking if we have seen their wives, or husbands, or children. We'll try to get to you when we can. Where are you?" she said.

Joanie tried to explain the highway number and location.

"I can't be exactly sure," Joanie said "I wasn't paying attention before the accident."

"We'll try to help," the operator said, hanging up in frustration.

Both Joanie and Meg were sobbing uncontrollably.

"Where can Natalie be?" cried Joanie again. "She was there, and then all of a sudden, she wasn't there! Have we gone mad?" she asked Meg.

"I don't know, Joanie, I was sort of dozing off in the back of the car. Joanie, this is like a scene out of a horror movie. Look at all the people standing on the road, all the cars that have crashed."

Strangely enough, there were other cars passing them on the road, as if nothing had happened. No one stopped to help. "Why aren't they in a ditch or on the side of the road like the others?" Joanie asked herself. Her head was spinning.

"Meg, can I have your cellphone? Mine is almost out of battery. I'm going to try and call my parents. Can you look after Mary?"

"Okay," Meg said.

Joanie fumbled with the phone. With her shaking hands, she could hardly dial the number. The phone on the other end rang—four, five, six rings—finally her mother answered.

"Mom!" Joanie wailed, "How are you? We've had a terrible thing happen here on the road."

Her mother interrupted:

"Joanie, we've been so worried about you. We tried to call you but no one answered the phone. Where exactly are you? What has happened?"

"Mom, I don't know where we are. I mean, we're on Highway 40 heading to Asheville, but something terrible happened!" She began to cry even more.

"Natalie was driving and the rest of us were taking a nap—all of a sudden the car went out of control. I was in the front passenger seat and I reached over to grab the steering wheel, and then, oh, Mom, I can't believe it. Nat wasn't there. She was just gone. I was panicked—no one was driving the car. I put my left foot over onto the brake, but the car crashed into the ditch on the side of the road. Meg and Mary were really hurt."

"Mom, what's going on, do you know? What are we going to do?"

"Joanie," her mother interrupted. "Listen to me! Something disastrous has happened. Your dad and I have had the TV on for the last hour. No one has any explanations, but millions of people, it seems, have disappeared around the world—just suddenly, in an instant. Nobody knows where they are or where they've gone!"

She continued:

"Oh, honey, planes have crashed around the world and all over the U.S. Pilots and passengers are missing; control tower operators are missing and the planes that are flying are not getting landing instructions. I mean," she said, "we've just been hearing all this on the news."

Joanie groaned.

"What's more," her mother continued with a terror-stricken voice, "cars have crashed all over the country, their drivers missing—they just disappeared, like you said about Natalie. We've been so afraid for you and the girls, honey."

"What else are the newscasters saying, Mom? Does anybody know what happened?" Joanie cried.

"No, some people have some ideas, like maybe that Jesus came back and took believers away as it talks about in the Bible, but no one is for sure," her mother responded.

"Even more disturbing, Joanie, a U.S. Senator was just on the news saying the Senate and House had been in session when suddenly, people were missing in both houses of Congress. There was mass confusion in the hall, he said. No one knew what to do. The pentagon had reported people missing from the Department of Defense, and other offices of government. Cities were in chaos, too, with firemen, policemen, school teachers, students, all kinds of people, just disappearing."

"Mom, is it the end of the world—I mean, what else could it be—there's no other explanation!?"

Her mother broke down in tears, finally handing the phone to Joanie's father.

"Oh, honey! We're so glad to hear from you and know you're safe! The world is in chaos—you must be very careful! No one knows what will happen next!"

"Dad, do you really think maybe Jesus came back and took people away? Nat had just been talking to us about that in the car!"

"If what the commentators are saying is true, there are many people who openly professed Christ as Savior who are gone," he said breathlessly. "They just announced that some famous athletes known for their outspoken Christian faith actually disappeared while playing in their televised games today—Tim Tebow was playing quarterback in todays game when all this happened, and he suddenly vanished, along with some other players—and on another network, Bubba Watson was putting on the 18th green, and he just disappeared—his ball and putter lying on the ground, and he wasn't there! Just 'in the twinkling of an eye,' these people are missing. It's incredible!"

"Oh, Dad!" Joanie cried. "It seems like the people that loved Jesus are gone and the rest of us are left behind! What do we do?"

"I don't know, Joanie. I'm just so sorry that I didn't take you and your mother to church all these years to learn more about Jesus and the Bible. I guess I didn't think it was that important, but now I know it was more important than anything. I'm so sorry," he cried. "Please forgive me."

"Of course I forgive you, Dad! I love you and mother so much!"

"I know. We love you, too, honey. We're so sorry we aren't there to help you. I know you have to go, but your mother wants to tell you one more thing quickly."

"Joanie, we just received a phone call before yours. It was from the hospital. You know our dearest friend, Maxine, has been in the hospital for several weeks. We loved her so much. She was such a kind and generous person and loved God with all her heart. She isn't there anymore either—along with many of the other patients, and doctors, and medical staff. They're all gone!"

Joanie thought about Natalie. She loved God, too. She was gone now—and then she again remembered Nat's words:

"I want you all to know Jesus, too. It's the most important decision you'll ever make. And Jesus is coming back someday soon—you're my best friends—I want you to be ready for His coming."

"That's, okay, Nat! We have plenty of time to talk about it…"

Luke 12:40
"Be ye therefore ready also; for the Son of man cometh
at an hour when ye think not."

I Thessalonians 4:15-18
"For this we say to you by the word of the Lord, that we
who are alive and remain until the coming of the Lord will
by no means precede those who are asleep.
For the Lord Himself will descend from heaven with a
shout, with the voice of an archangel, and with the trumpet
of God.. And the dead in Christ will rise first.
Then we who are alive and remain shall be caught up
together with them in the clouds to meet the Lord in the air.
And thus we shall always be with the Lord.
Therefore comfort one another with these words."

THE ULTIMATE QUESTION

In Matthew 24:14, the disciples asked Jesus:
"What will be the sign of your coming
and when will the end be?"

Jesus responded and said:

"There will be famines, wars and rumors of wars,
earthquakes, pestilence, men's hearts failing them for
fear, the sea and waves roaring, persecution of Christians,
violence, signs in the earth and heavens,
fierce and perilous times."

But the ultimate sign is this:
Matthew 24: 14
"This gospel of the kingdom will be preached in
all the world as a witness to all the nations,
and then the end will come."

Today, the gospel of Jesus Christ is penetrating every
corner of the world as NEVER before. Through
television, internet, radio, movies, Bibles, books,
missionaries, evangelists, and individual evangelism,
the time of His coming is nigh at the door.

The Ultimate Question is:

Are you ready to meet God?

Jesus said,
"Unless one is born again he cannot see the
kingdom of God." (John 3:3)
This new birth happens when you believe with your heart,
mind and will, that Christ died for your sins and accept by
faith His offer of forgiveness and new life.

2 Corinthians 6:2 states that
"Now is the accepted time, now is the day of salvation."
No one knows the exact hour or day when their life will
end or when Christ will return.

Jesus warns in Matthew 24:44
"Therefore, you also be ready, for the Son of Man is
coming at an hour you do not expect."

Today is your opportunity to accept Christ as your Savior
and Lord. You may use the following prayer,
or words of your own:

Lord Jesus, I believe that you are truly the Son of God.
I confess that I have sinned against you and I ask you to
forgive my sins and make me a new person.
I receive you now as my personal Savior.
Thank you for saving me and help me to live
a life that is pleasing to you.
In Christ's name I pray.
Amen

2 Corinthians 5,:17 "Therefore, if anyone is in Christ, he
is a new creature; old things are passed away, Behold, all
things become new."

I THESSALONIANS 4:11-17

ACCORDING TO THE LORD'S OWN WORD
"FOR THE LORD HIMSELF WILL COME DOWN
FROM HEAVEN, WITH A LOUD COMMAND,
WITH THE VOICE OF THE ARCHANGEL AND
WITH THE TRUMPET CALL OF GOD,
AND THE DEAD IN CHRIST WILL RISE FIRST.
AFTER THAT, WE WHO ARE STILL ALIVE AND ARE
LEFT WILL BE CAUGHT UP TOGETHER WITH THEM
IN THE CLOUDS TO MEET THE LORD IN THE AIR.
AND SO WE WILL BE WITH THE LORD FOREVER."

Diane Bish

Diane Bish is the most visible and influential classical organist performing today. Concert and recording artist, composer, conductor, and international television personality, Diane Bish displays her dazzling virtuosity and unique showmanship the world over to international acclaim. Her organ performances are hailed as "stunning, virtuoso, fiery, and astonishing."

Miss Bish's unparalleled achievements as a young performer gave her the credibility and determination to launch The Joy of Music international television series in 1982 as a platform for awareness and appreciation of "the king of instruments." Broadcast to over 300 million people around the world each week, The Joy of Music combines exhilarating organ and ensemble performances with an informative, inspirational narrative and exciting world travel. The Joy of Music boasts over 500 episodes featuring famous cathedrals, concert halls, churches and organs. This tremendous outreach to the general public on behalf of the organ and Diane Bish's longevity as a leading recitalist distinguishes her in the world of music.

In 1989, Miss Bish was awarded the National Citation by the National Federation of Music Clubs of America. Considered to be the Federation's highest honor, Diane Bish shares this rare distinction with such legends as Leonard Bernstein, Eugene Ormandy, Van Cliburn, Robert Shaw, Irving Berlin and Fred Waring in receiving this award "for distinguished service to the musical, artistic, and cultural life of the nation."

A consummate church musician, Diane Bish served as senior organist and artist-in-residence at the Coral Ridge

Presbyterian Church in Fort Lauderdale, Florida, for over 20 years. While at Coral Ridge Church, she led the design of the 117-rank Ruffatti organ, distinguished as one of the great organs in America. She was instrumental in developing one of the country's first church concert series and creating an annual church music workshop for musicians around the world. In her book Church Music Explosion, Miss Bish shares her philosophy of excellence in church music.

Miss Bish has recorded on the foremost organs of the world and was the first American woman to record on the four organs of Freiburg Cathedral, Germany. Featured on over 30 of her recordings are music for organ and orchestra, brass and organ, great organ masterpieces, organ and harp, original works, and hymn arrangements.

The sparkling creativity and artistry of Diane Bish is equally evident in her compositions. She has composed numerous solo pieces, arrangements, and full chorale & symphonic works that have received much acclaim and are performed regularly due to her ability to combine musical quality with accessibility.

Her list of creative projects also includes the Diane Bish Signature Series by Allen line of digital organs. Working closely with the technicians and designers at <u>Allen Organ Company</u>, Miss Bish beautifully combined her musical vision and expertise with the superior technical design of the Allen Organ. Many Diane Bish Signature Series Organs have been installed around the country and are available through the <u>Allen Organ Company</u>.

Diane Bish began her study with Dorothy Addy in Wichita, Kansas, and continued as a student of Mildred Andrews. She was a recipient of Fulbright and French government grants for study in Amsterdam and Paris with Nadia Boulanger, Gustav Leonhardt and Marie Claire Alain. <u>Diane Bish: First Lady of the Organ</u> by Warren Woodruff was published in 1993.

For more information on Diane Bish & The Joy of Music
and to purchase DVDs and CDs, please contact:

The Joy of Music
PO Box 5564
Bloomington, IN 47407

Phone: 1-800-933-4844
Email: joymusic.jom@gmail.com
Web: www.thejoyofmusic.org

To host a Diane Bish Concert, please contact:

Janet Jarriel
JEJ Artists
218 Wimbledon Place
Macon, GA 31211

Phone: 404-663-4135
Email: janet@jejartists.com
Web: www.jejartists.com

CD and DVD packages
by Diane Bish

HYMNS AND CLASSICS

CLASSICAL ORGAN FAVORITES

ENCORE

SACRED FAVORITES FOR HARP AND ORGAN

JOY TO THE WORLD FOR HARP AND ORGAN

GREAT EUROPEAN ORGANS

CHRISTMAS FAVORITES FOR BRASS AND ORGAN

FAVORITES FROM FREIBURG CATHEDRAL,
    GERMANY

MORNING HAS BROKEN, A SYMPHONY OF HYMNS
    FOR organ, choir and orchestra

SACRED FAVORITES for Soprano and organ

DVD PACKAGES

MUSICAL JOURNEYS OF FRANCE
MUSICAL JOURNEYS OF GERMANY
MUSICAL JOURNEYS OF SWITZERLAND
MUSICAL JOURNEYS OF HOLLAND
MUSICAL JOURNEYS OS AUSTRIA
MUSICAL JOURNEYS OF THE UNITED KINGDOM
MUSICAL JOURNEYS OF SCANDANAVIA

A EUROPEAN CHRISTMAS
CHRISTMAS ON THE DANUBE
CHRISTMAS IN GERMANY
CHRISTMAS FAVORITES FROM GREAT AMERICAN
CHURCHES AND ORGANS

GREAT MOMENTS OF CHRISTMAS
CHRISTMAS AT BILTMORE

GREAT MOMENTS OF THE JOY OF MUSIC
MEMORABLE MOMENTS OF THE JOY OF MUSIC

MUSIC AND THE BIBLE

GREAT COMPOSERS

MUSIC OF JOHANN SEBASTIAN BACH
GREAT COMPOSERS

GREAT HYMNS OF FAITH
HYMNS AND GOSPEL SONGS
SACRED FAVORITES

CPSIA information can be obtained at www.ICGtesting.com
Printed in the USA
LVOW060859060213

318790LV00002B/3/P